BRAIN BUILDER
NUMBERS

BRAIN BUILDER
NUMBERS

Charles Phillips

**PUZZLE
WRIGHT
PRESS**

New York

Charles Phillips would like to dedicate this book to Jim: a clear thinker.

PUZZLE
WRIGHT
PRESS

New York

An Imprint of Sterling Publishing
387 Park Avenue South
New York, NY 10016

Text and puzzles copyright © 2011 by Bibelot Limited
Published by arrangement with Eddison Sadd Editions Limited, London

ISBN 978-1-4549-0032-0

Distributed in Canada by Sterling Publishing
C/o Canadian Manda Group, 165 Dufferin Street
Toronto, Ontario, Canada M6K 3H6

For information about custom editions, special sales, and premium and corporate purchases,
please contact Sterling Special Sales at 800-805-5489 or specialsales@sterlingpublishing.com.

Manufactured in the United States of America

2 4 6 8 10 9 7 5 3 1

www.puzzlewright.com

CONTENTS

SECOND TEST 55

SECOND TEST ANSWERS 81

INTRODUCTION

The modern world frequently requires us to be confident in handling numbers. Although we have access to pocket calculators and to calculating software on our smartphones, laptops, and desktop computers, we still encounter situations in which doing a little mental mathematics is the key to appearing smart while thinking on your feet.

Perhaps you're a businessperson discussing invoices with your boss, or an advisor having to compare percentages for clients in a discussion about interest rates or pension funds. You might be out there in the world of politics—a member of a group of lobbyists debating ratios relevant to climate change, say, or challenging statistics when trying to protect your local library or children's center from funding cuts. Or you could be a student or a teacher in an academic discussion about an esoteric subject seemingly far removed from mathematics—the frequency of use of a particular phrase or word in Renaissance literature, say.

Equally, you might just be having fun! You could be calculating the odds on a horse or working out the tip in a restaurant, or in the supermarket deciding whether a special offer is really any cheaper.

Yet for all that we are called on to use numbers so frequently, many people have a persistent problem with arithmetic. Perhaps they were put off math at school by staid lessons and rote learning—some may have been told, or have decided, that they are "no good" at mathematics and now feel they are always likely to have difficulty with numbers.

The fact is, developing your number skills will help you in many situations in everyday life. We can all benefit enormously from building our numeracy and understanding the grammar of numbers. But don't panic! I am not suggesting a return to times tables and to doing sums, or urging you to commit to lots of hard work. The puzzles in this and the other books of the *Brain Builder* series (see page 13) are designed to be enjoyable and engaging. Why? Scientists tell us our brains work best when we're interested in what we're doing.

Where do numbers come from?

It seems that our ancestors developed counting as a way to track patterns in their experiences. One of the world's oldest mathematical artifacts, dated to 35,000 B.C.E., is a piece of baboon bone cut with 29 marks and found in the Lebombo Mountains of southern Africa. The marks are believed to represent the 29 nights of the moon's cycle.

Early people lived for millennia as hunters and gatherers. They needed to keep count of days and nights in order to track the waxing and waning of the moon and recurring changes in the seasons. When their descendants began farming around 10,000 B.C.E., they progressed from early calendars to recording numbers of animals and produce by scratching marks on tally sticks, collecting and counting pebbles, or making knots in a string.

After writing was invented, by the Sumerians of Mesopotamia in modern Iraq circa 3300 B.C.E., people began to write numbers down on clay or stone tablets, on walls and monuments, and on papyrus rolls. They used a wide variety of marks—the ancient Maya and Aztecs of Central America used lines and dots, while the Sumerians and others in Mesopotamia used nail- and chevron-shaped signs. The Hebrews, ancient Greeks, and (later) the ancient Romans used letters of the alphabet.

Art of numbers

The word "arithmetic" comes from the ancient Greek *arithmos* ("number") and *techne* ("craft" or "skill") and means the art (or skill) of handling numbers. When we do arithmetic we use tools such as subtraction, addition, division, and multiplication to investigate the qualities and behavior of numbers.

Most historians agree that people did not make their first breakthroughs in arithmetic until the civilizations of Mesopotamia, ancient Egypt, and the Indus Valley (Pakistan) in the third millennium B.C.E. However, some point to an African animal bone from 20,000 B.C.E. as evidence that many millennia earlier people understood the processes of doubling and halving—and even used prime numbers.

The bone, from Ishango on the border between Uganda and Congo, is marked with cuts in groups. One group has three and six, four and eight, ten and five cuts—indicating familiarity with doubles and halves. Another group has the prime numbers 11, 13, 7, and 19. There is also a group containing 11, 9, 21, and 19 (10 + 1, 10 − 1, 20 + 1, 20 − 1). It's possible that, like the Lebombo bone, the Ishango bone was a calendar. Of course, it may be that the prime numbers appear by coincidence—we have no other indications that people knew about prime numbers before the time of the ancient Greeks. Yet some believe that more than 20,000 years ago Africans were using mathematical aids to make fairly complex numerical calculations.

The numbers we know

Our familiar numerals—1, 2, 3, 4, 5, 6, 7, 8, 9, and 0—are called Arabic numerals because they came into use in Europe by way of Arabic scientists active in North Africa and Islamic Spain. The numbers were introduced into Italy, and from there into France and Germany, by the Italian mathematician Leonardo of Pisa (c.1170–c.1250) in his book *Liber Abaci* ("Book of the Abacus," 1202). At that time, most of Europe, apart from Islamic Spain, counted using Roman numerals such as I (for 1), V (5), X (10), L (50), C (100), and so on.

The Arabic numerals had actually been developed by Indian mathematicians circa 400 B.C.E., then adopted by Persian and Arabic scientists. Leonardo learned of the numbers and system while living with his father, a merchant, in the territory of the Muslim Almohad dynasty in North Africa.

Leonardo is also known as Fibonacci. He is associated with the Fibonacci sequence of numbers—a progression, starting with 0 and 1, in which each number is the sum of the previous two. The sequence begins 0, 1, 1, 2, 3, 5, 8, 13, 21, 34, 55. He described the sequence in the "Book of the Abacus." We look at the Fibonacci sequence in more detail in *Brain Builder: Sequences*.

Position matters

In the "Book of the Abacus," Leonardo also introduced the positional decimal system used by the Arabs (and before them the Indians) to Italy, from where it passed with the Arabic numerals to France and Germany. This is the familiar system in which the first 1 in 111 stands for 1 hundred, the second for 1 ten, and the third for 1 unit. It's called the positional system because a number's value depends on its position, and decimal (from the Latin *decimus*, "tenth") because it has a base of ten—a 1 in the second position stands for a 10. The system was developed and first used in India in the 5th century c.e. There were other positional systems. The Babylonians of Mesopotamia, for example, used a sexagesimal system—it had a base of sixty rather than ten. (The number 30 in base 60, for example, equals 180 in base ten). The Maya of Central America had a vigesimal system—with a base of twenty.

To work really well, positional systems depend on the idea of zero. You can't write 101 for "one hundred one" without being able to write zero in the tens column. But the representation of zero differed from culture to culture. The Babylonians, for example, did not have a zero; they used a space (and later two wedge symbols) to indicate nothing in a column. The oldest surviving evidence of people using 0 as a digit is from the 9th century c.e.

Only two numbers needed

Your laptop or desktop computer, your digital TV, and your cellphone make do with only two of the Arabic numerals: 0 and 1. The system works very

• •

well for electrical machines such as these: 1 means "electrical current on," and 0 means "current off." In mathematical terms, computer language uses a binary base system: While in the decimal system the 1 in 10 stands for one 10, in a binary base system the 1 in 10 stands for one 2, 100 stands for 4, and so on. In this system 11 stands for 3 and 111 stands for 7. What does 1,000 stand for? And what about 1,111? (Answers: 1,000 = 8, and 1,111 = 15.)

The German mathematician and philosopher Gottfried Leibniz (1646–1716) argued that we should use a binary base system with 1s and 0s. He believed it could be part of a new (mathematical) language to be used for making exact statements of logical thought, and that this language would be free of the ambiguities of tone and meaning found in verbal language.

Whole and broken, rational and irrational

Fractions are numbers that come between whole numbers. They take their name from the Latin *fractio* ("breaking"). Between 0 and 1, say, there is a progression of fractions: ½, ¼, ⅛, and so on. This goes on forever since you can always divide a fraction—for example, 1⁄16, 1⁄32, 1⁄64....

Fractions are rational numbers; any whole number or any number that can be written as a ratio of two whole numbers is called a rational number. Some numbers cannot be written as fractions. These are called irrational numbers. A celebrated example is π (pi, named for the ancient Greek equivalent of our letter "p"). Pi is the ratio of a circle's circumference to its diameter. It is approximately 22⁄7, but cannot be written exactly.

Another way to express fractions is with the decimal system. In this system ½ (equivalent to 5⁄10) is written 0.5; ¼ (equivalent to 25⁄100) is 0.25—and so on. Some rational decimals cannot be written as finite numbers; their digits recur. For instance, ⅓ is 0.3333… with the 3's recurring to infinity. All irrational numbers expressed as decimals extend infinitely, but their numbers do not recur; for instance, π begins 3.1415926535... and continues unpredictably to infinity.

THINK BETTER

Numbers are *the* international language. If I close my eyes and type randomly, I come up with this: "hhhewhsdsh." In other words, gibberish. But if I do the same thing on my keyboard's number pad, I get (for example) 24579434. This is the notation for twenty-four million, five hundred seventy-nine thousand, four hundred thirty-four. In other words, in our positional decimal system, every combination of digits has a meaning. Even if I type only zeros—as here, 000000—the number still has mathematical meaning. Arabic numerals, although not the only number system in the world, are understood very widely and in diverse cultures—and, as such, they represent an international language. So, when it comes to numbers, we all speak the same language.

If you struggle with numbers, the quality of your thinking could be compromised, and that could affect your performance at work, in college, in interviews, socially, or in any other aspect of your everyday life. What if you're suddenly faced with a situation that requires quick numerical thinking? You might have to give an immediate decision in relation to a business offer or in a discussion about salary or benefits. How well you cope will depend to a large extent on your brain's ability to identify salient points quickly and clearly, to see connections and process facts—another reason to make sure your brain is up to speed.

If you have difficulties with numbers from time to time, this is nothing to be ashamed of. We all have different strengths and problematic areas, and one key to success is to identify our weaknesses and set to work to build our brain performance. This is where the puzzles in *Brain Builder: Numbers* come in. This collection of puzzles provides key guidance on how to cope effectively with numerical problems, together with a wealth of practical advice and insights to enable improved confidence with numbers.

Not only that, you can go on to tackle the puzzles in the other three volumes (see opposite)—helping you to become a good all-around thinker.

· ·

USE THIS BOOK TO IMPROVE YOUR THINKING

Numbers is one of four titles in the *Brain Builder* series (see below). All four provide an enjoyable two-stage mental workout that enables you to measure your capacity for a type of thinking, then set to work at once to improve your performance as necessary.

In each book there are two series of puzzles: the First Test and the Second Test. The answer section for each test follows directly after it. As you complete the puzzles and challenges in the First Test, use the scoring system to measure your ability for that theme (see "How to Score Your Performance" on page 14). Then, in the expanded First Test answer section, you can soak up the hints, tips, and guidance that will prepare you for the fresh challenges in the Second Test.

Take stock, then prepare to work through the Second Test, scoring your answers and comparing the totals for both tests to establish whether and how your ability for that theme has improved. Don't worry if you find your overall score hasn't increased—it's a guide only. What matters is that you start thinking about and understanding the processes involved.

Next, tackle the themes in the other three volumes of the *Brain Builder* series (*Sequences*, *Patterns*, and *Shapes*) and gain a picture of your brain's overall performance (see also the scoring chart on pages 90–91). You can then focus on the types of thinking that you need to build on first if you want to improve further. What's more, you'll soon see how this improvement can raise the quality of your thinking wherever you are and whatever you're doing—whether at work, studying, socializing, or just relaxing.

Before you start, be sure to tackle the cover puzzle (instructions are on the next page; the solution is on page 89). And remember that you'll find Notes and Scribbles pages on pages 93–95 where you can do your calculations.

The *Brain Builder* titles can help you change your habits of thinking and perception to make a real difference in your everyday life. Have fun!

COVER PUZZLE INSTRUCTIONS

To solve the cover as an interactive puzzle, make a copy and cut it into seven hexagons (as shown at right). The goal is to rearrange the hexagons without rotating them and write numbers in the empty circles so that the numbers on each hexagon add up to the same total, and pairs of adjacent triangles multiply to the same product. For a greater challenge, try solving the puzzle in your head, without cutting out the pieces.

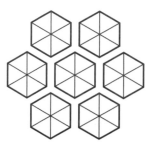

HOW TO SCORE YOUR PERFORMANCE

If you get an answer correct, award yourself 2 points. In some cases you may find that you didn't quite solve the puzzle, but you were clearly working along the right lines—in this case, award yourself 1 point. If, however, your whole approach was wrong or you couldn't see a way to answer the question at all, you score 0.

In the first answer section there's advice, background information, and Brain Builder Tips to help you improve your performance in any areas you find difficult. In some cases, I have provided an opportunity later to have a second or even a third go at a certain type of puzzle. This gives you a chance to try out the effectiveness of the tips and advice.

BRAIN BUILDER
NUMBERS

FIRST TEST

Try your hand at the twenty-five puzzles in the First Test. They are of varying degrees of difficulty—ten standard difficulty, ten medium difficulty, and five tricky. As you go, score your performance, following the guidance on page 14. Don't forget that the answer section contains advice to help you raise your performance. Good luck—and, above all, enjoy yourself!

PUZZLE 1 SIX OF FIVE

An ecologically conscious architect comes up with this pentagon number puzzle while designing a cluster of "green" classrooms. The task is to discover the mathematical pattern behind the numbers on these pentagons and fill in the blank faces to complete the puzzle.

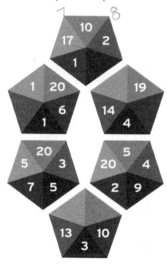

You need to work out the relationship between numbers and within groups of numbers, thereby developing your mathematical facility and confidence.

BRAIN BUILDER CLUE Look for the places where the pentagons are fully aligned face-to-face.

PUZZLE 2 SWEET ADDITIONS

Gazing at three elegant piles of sugar-dusted bonbons, an alert patisserie worker comes up with this simple addition challenge. The number in each circle is the sum of the two numbers in the circles underneath it: Can you fill in the rest of the blanks and complete the three pyramids?

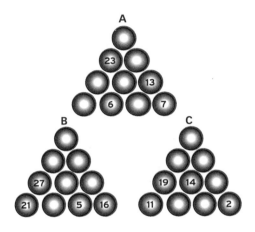

This is a simple test of arithmetic, although there may be a couple of places where you have to work backward from a total to its constituent numbers. How quickly can you do it? Doing fairly easy number challenges as quickly as you can works well as a warmup for more challenging number puzzles.

Try working up the right-hand side of pyramid A then down the left-hand side.

17

PUZZLE 3 FOUR SQUARE AT THE NUMERO UNO

The barman in the Numero Uno bar does not encourage his customers to count their drinks too carefully, but he does use nifty numbered beer mats in shapes designed to appeal to math-lovers. One quiet evening he comes up with this mini challenge. The value of a shape is the number of sides the shape has, multiplied by the number within it (so, a triangle containing a 4 would have a value of 12). Can you find a block of four squares—two squares wide by two squares high—with a total value of 30?

This puzzle combines an element of visual thinking with a numerical challenge, making it a real Brain Builder. The combined visual-numerical challenge engages diverse parts of the brain, and scientists tell us that activities that engage several brain areas at once really boost mental performance.

BRAIN BUILDER **CLUE**   Avoid high numbers in shapes of many sides.

PUZZLE 4 PILLOW SUMS

At the Puzzlers' Hotel, the staff leaves cross-number puzzles like this on top of the pillows in guests' newly cleaned rooms. The task is to find the right locations in the grid for all of the listed numbers.

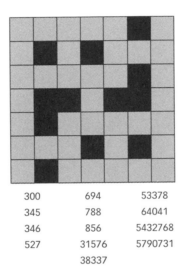

300	694	53378
345	788	64041
346	856	5432768
527	31576	5790731
	38337	

Demonstrate your ingenuity with combinations of numbers by beating this grid challenge.

Whichever order the two longest numbers go in the grid, there are some squares that will be the same no matter what.

19

PUZZLE 5 ANTARCTIC NUMBERS

A mathematics and computing teacher devises this "Antarctic Numbers" video game for her students. Each player takes the form of a penguin and starts at the top left with the number provided: He or she then works from one steppingstone to the next, applying the mathematical instructions to the running total. Any mistakes cause the steppingstone to sink into the freezing waters, and the player must start again. What answer do you get?

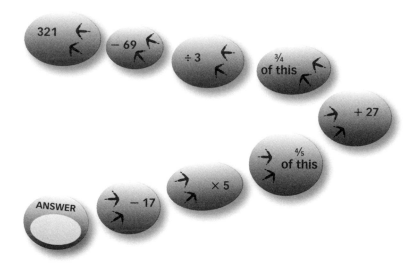

No calculators or pencil and paper, please! This exercise works best if you do all the required arithmetic in your head.

BRAIN BUILDER **CLUE** Don't forget simple strategies like rounding up or down. Say you have to add 23 + 59; it's easier to add 23 + 60, then subtract 1. This trick will come in handy at the start here.

PUZZLE 6 ARITHMARACE!

To pass time before a big race at the track meet, a sprinter creates this speedy challenge for his colleagues in the relay team. The task is to work through the fifteen number-crunching questions before the 2-minute time limit elapses.

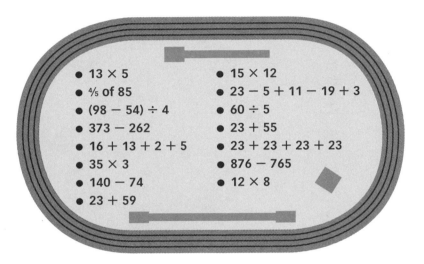

- 13 × 5
- ⅘ of 85
- (98 − 54) ÷ 4
- 373 − 262
- 16 + 13 + 2 + 5
- 35 × 3
- 140 − 74
- 23 + 59
- 15 × 12
- 23 − 5 + 11 − 19 + 3
- 60 ÷ 5
- 23 + 55
- 23 + 23 + 23 + 23
- 876 − 765
- 12 × 8

The athlete threw in a couple of straightforward times-tables questions to speed you on your way. Working through these questions—and as quickly as you can—makes you focus. No bad thing for members of a team of relay runners, who can't afford any blunders!

BRAIN BUILDER CLUE
A tip for speed in dealing with larger subtraction sums: Simply look at the difference between the digits in each column—that is, differences in the units, tens, and hundreds columns.

PUZZLE 7 HOW MUCH ARE THEY WORTH?

Four wealthy couples seated on a restaurant's patio linger long into the night, and so the headwaiter has time to dream up this number puzzle. Each of the eight sections of the table, A–H, contains a different number between 1 and 20. See if you can work them all out from the information below.

- $C - F = A$
- B squared = D
- $B + G + F = C$
- $H - (A + G) = E$
- $D = F \times E$
- F squared = B
- G is one-eighth of $(D + E)$

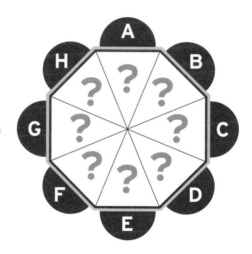

You need to think logically to work out what values are feasible. Keep track of which numbers have been firmly identified so you can eliminate them as possibilities for other letters.

BRAIN BUILDER CLUE Only three numbers besides 1 can be squared (multiplied by themselves) to produce a number less than 20. That means not many values will work for F, B, and D.

PUZZLE 8 BID SERIES

At the auction house, an intern creates this number-sequence game with tickets used to identify lots for auction. In her game, the arrows indicate whether a number in a box is greater than or less than an adjacent number. Can you do it? You have to complete the grid so that each of the rows and columns contains the numbers 1–5 exactly once each.

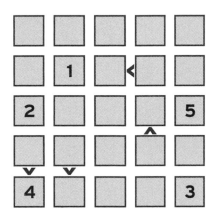

If you've ever solved sudoku, you can use similar logic in this puzzle to identify and eliminate possibilities.

You have enough information provided to fill in the first column right away.

PUZZLE 9 GIVE US A SIGN

The monks in the monastery play this game on days when they're keeping a vow of silence. They write numbers on a blackboard and raise cards with the mathematical symbols +, −, ×, or ÷ to make the given total. Can you help them with today's problems? The rules are:

- Use three of the four symbols above in each problem.
- Don't create fractions or numbers less than zero at any step.
- Solve from left to right.

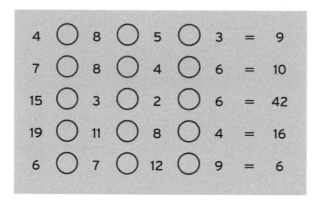

Once again you need common sense. Generally, you'll want to keep the multiplication symbol away from the larger numbers—otherwise you'll create some unwieldy totals!

PUZZLE 10 FARE'S FAIR IN NUMEROVILLE

In the video game "Numeroville" you have to pass this Find the Totals challenge in order to gain a lucrative registration as a taxi driver. In each line of the number sheet, below, one number is the sum of two others—how quickly can you spot each one?

14	24	7	34	11	55	8	2	97	73
101	202	305	69	404	506	32	907	31	68
39	41	53	63	82	93	124	118	33	72
3	2	6	30	15	14	25	82	86	24
791	917	717	919	91	19	999	99	882	1097

You need to be alert and quick-witted to spot the connections. As we've seen in other puzzles, the more familiar you are with number combinations—the more frequently you think about and play around with numbers—the better you'll do.

BRAIN BUILDER CLUE At least one of the pair of numbers to be added together to make the bigger number can be found within the first four options in each row.

PUZZLE 11 PUZZLING PEANUTS AT THE SHERLOCK HOLMES

Clients at the Sherlock Holmes bar can buy the bar's own brand of snacks, called "Elementary," which come in brain-tickling puzzle wrappings. Can you solve this example, found on a bag of peanuts? The task is to place the digits 1–9 in the white squares so it's possible to jump in sequence from one digit to the next, using only the steps indicated in the eight diamond shapes. The digits in each diamond indicate distance and direction traveled from one number to the next. For instance, the lower left diamond indicates a move one square up. Some numbers are already placed.

- Each diamond step must be used exactly once.
- Both parts of a two-part step must be used, but may be taken in either order.
- No part of any step may pass over a shaded square.

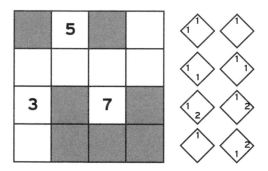

This is principally a logic puzzle. You're relying on clarity of thinking as you visualize the number positions that will fit with the possible moves supplied.

 There's only one place in the grid you can travel down two spaces.

PUZZLE 12 AGENT 8

An ability to do arithmetic quickly and accurately is one of many qualities needed by special agents—hence this number challenge from the video game "Agent 8." Players have to complete the two number columns within a time limit before passing on to a bomb-defusing challenge at the next level. Could you make it as a special agent? Start with the number given, then follow the sums from top to bottom to reach two answers.

Easy	Tough
5	**5**
Add 44	Multiply by 9
Divide by 7	Add 153
Add 74	Divide by 3
Divide by 3	Halve it
Minus 3	Square it
Multiply by 4	Divide by 9
Double it	Multiply by 3
Minus 44	Minus 27
Divide by 37	Divide by 28

Tests of speed calculation like this require accuracy and confidence. Set yourself a time limit—say, 2 minutes—to complete the puzzle.

BRAIN BUILDER
CLUE

If you go into four figures at "Square it" in the second column you're on the right track.

27

PUZZLE 13 28 CAKES

Our patisserie (Puzzle 2) supplies this Cake Mountain for a math professor's
28th anniversary party. The numbers given are drawn in icing, and party guests
have to add the missing numbers to the other cakes. No one is allowed to eat
any of the cakes before all the numbers are filled in, so they're understandably
in a hurry. Can you help them? There's just one simple rule to keep in mind:

- The number on each cake is the sum of the two numbers on the cakes
  beneath it.

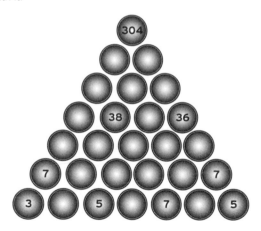

*As in Puzzle 2, try setting yourself a time limit (1 minute?) to work through this
simple arithmetic test without a calculator. You'll know if you make a mistake
because you have to finish with numbers that total 304 at the top.*

The best place to start is probably at the bottom right. Don't get stuck
trying to fill the puzzle line by line—as we noted in Puzzle 2, sometimes you
have to work back down from higher numbers to plug some gaps.

PUZZLE 14 IT'S ELEMENTARY

A detective sets a logic-pattern puzzle like this for his partner at the agency once or twice a week to test and develop his powers of deduction. Can you help with this one? The question is: If the grid follows a logical pattern, what should occupy the squares A, B, and C?

This requires you to identify patterns across the grid in terms of shading and numbers. You need to look closely and think clearly to count squares and assess the number relationships.

Can you make the patterns add up?

29

● ●

PUZZLE 15 TIME IN NUMBERS

In a time-travel video game the player has to work out the correct answer to this mental mathematics challenge in order to escape from the year 1000 back to the present.

The task is to multiply the number of days in the week by the number of hours in a day, then add the number of weeks in a year before multiplying by the number of years in a century; then subtract the number of minutes in a day and add the number of months in a decade before finally adding the number of years between the present and the year 1000.

Definitely no calculators allowed! For a really "aerobic" brain workout try to complete this number challenge as fast as you can while doing all the calculations in your head—without using pen and paper....

BRAIN BUILDER **CLUE**
You should find the first few steps easy, but if you're solving in your head, the tricky part will be remembering your running total as you calculate the number of minutes in a day or the number of months in a decade.

PUZZLE 16 NUMBER FITNESS

An actress's personal trainer designs number-fitness puzzles to complement her physical workouts and keep her mentally primed. In this challenge, the clues to this puzzle appear within the grid.

- Each blank square contains a single number from 1 to 9.
- Every set of numbers across or down has a total equal to that of its clue, shown either directly above or directly to the left (see the example grid on the left: 9 + 8 in the top line totals 17; 9 + 7 + 5 in the left-hand column totals 21—and so on).
- No digit may be duplicated within any set.

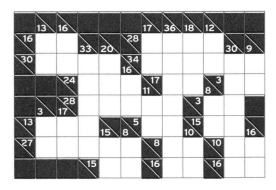

This is a Kakuro puzzle, named for Japanese words meaning "addition" and "cross." Kakuro are essentially number crosswords, and are sometimes laid out with the clues in a list like conventional crossword clues. They are good for developing your ability to see number combinations and interconnections.

BRAIN BUILDER CLUE: There's only one way to add two digits to make 16 without repeating a number, and only one way to add four digits to make 30 without repeats.

• •

PUZZLE 17 ODDS 'N' EVENS NUMBER TIPTOE

A designer creates this puzzle, which he calls a "Number Tiptoe," as a quick numerical challenge for a touch-screen smartphone. The task is to fill in the circles so that every row and column of six circles contains the numbers 1–6 exactly once each. The white circles can contain only odd numbers (1, 3, and 5), while the shaded circles can contain only even numbers (2, 4, and 6). Some numbers are already in place.

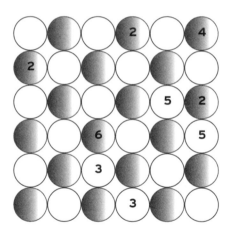

This puzzle requires you to think logically to balance rows and columns, odds and evens.

You'll solve more quickly if you focus on the odds and evens separately.

PUZZLE 18 THREE-WAY FIT

A playwright designs this puzzle to go in the program of his play *Three,* about a cranky widowed mathematician and his two sons. There are three ways in which you must fit numbers into the puzzle: Each row, each column, and each set of linked circles should contain the numbers 1–6 exactly once each.

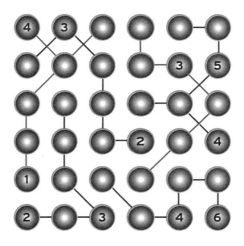

This provides an intriguing angle on sudoku-style puzzles, using chains rather than blocks of squares to group the numbers. You need the same combination of logic and visual intelligence you would use for a sudoku or for the Number Tiptoe puzzle on the opposite page.

Start with the six-digit chain containing a 4 and 6 at the bottom right: You have enough information supplied to fill most of this in right away.

33

PUZZLE 19 NUMBER BY NUMBERS

Wanting to hide crucial information from the police, a private detective encodes a message for his partner. The numbers adjacent to each row and column describe squares and groups of squares that are adjoining (if no numbers are given, no squares are colored in that row or column). Each group of squares must be separated from any groups in the same row or column by at least one empty square. Color in the grid correctly, and a six-digit combination will be revealed.

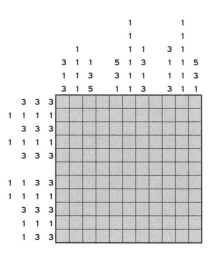

This requires attention to detail and use of visual logic. This is a type of puzzle known as Nonograms (among other names). Have a look at Brain Builder: Patterns *for further examples.*

From the blank rows and columns, we can tell that the six digits must be arranged in the grid in two rows of three.

PUZZLE 20 WEIGH IT UP

An assistant at an upscale butcher shop bases a puzzle for his girlfriend on the traditional scales he uses every day at work. In his puzzle, each of the five differently colored and patterned balls represents a different weight—1, 2, 3, 4, or 5 pounds. Can you work out which ball weighs what, and how many spotted balls will balance the final scale?

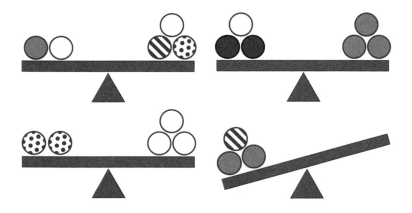

This is an elegant combination of numerical and visual elements. Can you read the coded weight of each colored/patterned ball, then balance the scales?

BRAIN BUILDER CLUE The first scale suggests that the weight furthest to the left must represent one of the higher numbers. (Note that you can cancel out the two white weights on either side of that scale.)

PUZZLE 21 SUM PEOPLE!

How much are they worth? A worker in a health-food cooperative draws this lighthearted grid featuring his four colleagues. Each character represents a different number, and the number at the end of each row and column represents the sum of all the numbers in that row or column. Can you work out which number each character represents, and determine what number should replace the question mark?

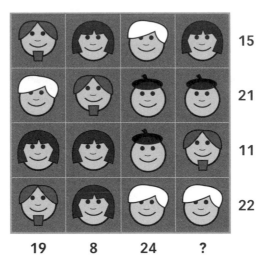

This is an entertaining decoding challenge. You'll have to use the logic of sums in deducing which numbers will work for this combination of faces.

The second column from the left suggests that the dark-haired woman's face must represent a low number.

PUZZLE 22 MAZE 4

An architectural author and maze expert designs this number-path puzzle as a gift to celebrate his fourth wedding anniversary. Can you solve it? Your task is to find your way from any square on the top row of the grid to any square on the bottom row, passing only through numbers that will divide exactly by 4. No diagonal moves are allowed.

36	22	78	70	30	40	12	13	52
40	94	96	80	16	54	30	77	72
42	74	48	54	76	64	44	68	92
60	56	28	22	98	86	18	22	36
80	69	12	30	40	36	32	62	52
84	78	20	88	24	46	72	50	64
92	38	22	90	66	34	96	34	70
16	24	32	28	50	38	76	16	56
22	46	14	82	94	82	62	26	88

This is a simple puzzle that tests quick thinking, your facility with numbers, and your attention to detail.

You could solve this by looking only for squares divisible by four and tracing a path that way, or by blacking out squares not divisible by four and treating them like the walls of a maze.

PUZZLE 23 HAPPY 49TH AT THE NUMERO UNO

The barman at the Numero Uno bar (Puzzle 3) sets up this number-path challenge for a regular customer's 49th birthday bash. The task is to place numbered beer mats in the grid so that the numbers 1–49 connect in a consecutively numbered path through adjacent squares horizontally, vertically, or diagonally in any direction, starting and ending in the indicated squares. Some numbers in the path are already provided.

20			17			4
	15	16	1		36	
	24			34		6
23				40		7
26		42			39	8
30			49	48		
	28				47	10

This is an example of a Hidato puzzle, an excellent exercise in numerical logic. The Hidato was developed by the Transylvanian-born Israeli computer scientist Dr. Gyora Benedek. He says he was inspired to create the puzzle by an encounter with a fast-moving shoal of small fish while he was scuba diving in the Red Sea; he wanted to re-create the fishes' darting movements in a puzzle.

BRAIN BUILDER
CLUE

There are two options for reaching the 4 in the top-right corner from your starting position at 1—but only one will allow you to complete the later 34-35-36 move.

PUZZLE 24 MENU NUMBERS

At the Puzzlers' Hotel (see Puzzle 4) the waiters often have a go at these cross-number puzzles, which are printed on menus and table napkins to entertain restless diners while they wait for their food. The task is to fit the following numbers into the crisscross grid.

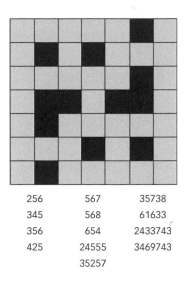

256	567	35738
345	568	61633
356	654	2433743
425	24555	3469743
	35257	

This is another test of your visual and numerical logic. Look for likely intersections among the numbers.

Note that the last three digits of both 7-digit numbers are the same.

39

PUZZLE 25 IN THE ZONE

A tennis player works on puzzles like this to make sure he is fully focused for his matches on the court. Can you solve this one? Your task is to place the numbers 1–9 once each in every row. Each arrow in the boxes outside of the grid tells you the total of the digits in the diagonal to which the arrow points.

- Numbers may appear multiple times in columns.
- Identical numbers may not appear in neighboring squares (even diagonally).

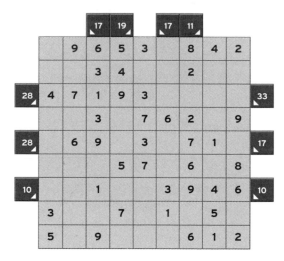

This puzzle will develop logical thinking and boost your confidence with numbers.

The short, two-square diagonal clues provide a good place to start.

FIRST TEST ANSWERS

Stop! Don't turn to the answer section too quickly—even if you find a puzzle hard to solve, it sometimes helps to take a break and return to it later. When you do look up the answer, make this part of your learning—study it, work out the method by which it was solved, then go back to the puzzle to understand the steps involved. Try to determine why and how the answer is correct. This section not only provides the answers to puzzles 1–25 in the First Test (pages 15–40) but also includes hints, tips, and guidance to prepare you for Puzzles 26–50 in the Second Test (pages 55–80). Absorb the extra information before you tackle the Second Test. It should help improve your brain power!

● ●

> Award yourself points as follows:
> ● Correct answer: **2 points** ● Wrong answer but on the right track: **1 point**
> ● Completely wrong answer or no answer at all: **0 points**

PUZZLE 1 SIX OF FIVE

The numbers on each pentagon add up to 40, while the numbers on facing sides of neighboring pentagons, when multiplied, equal 20.

BRAIN BUILDER TIP Playing around with addition and multiplication problems will further develop the numerical facility and confidence you need to do a puzzle like this. Consider a number—say, 6—and work out the numbers that divide exactly into it: 1, 2, 3, and 6 itself. These are called its divisors. 1, 2, and 3 also add up to 6; numbers like 6, whose divisors (not counting itself) add up to the original number, are called "perfect numbers." 28 is one too (its divisors are 1, 2, 4, 7, and 14). Can you work out the next one? It's quite a long way off on the number line! *(See the Brain Builder Tip for Puzzle 2 for the answer.)*

PUZZLE 2 SWEET ADDITIONS

The completed number pyramids are shown below.

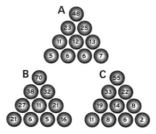

BRAIN BUILDER TIP There are many everyday occasions when you're called on to make simple calculations quickly. You might be buying a large order of coffees and teas for your coworkers; try keeping track of the total cost in your head, or calculating the change you'll be getting back after you pay. It's great to have the confidence that comes from an ability to handle number combinations without being at the mercy of the person serving you. *(Puzzle 1 answer: The next perfect number after 28 is 496. Its divisors are 1, 2, 4, 8, 16, 31, 62, 124, and 248.)*

POINTS

PUZZLE 3 FOUR SQUARE AT THE NUMERO UNO

The correct area is indicated below. It includes a square containing 3, giving a value of 12 (4 × 3 = 12); and three triangles containing 1, 2, and 3, respectively ([1 + 2 + 3] × 3 = 18). This adds up to our total (12 + 18 = 30).

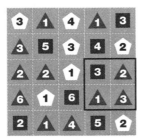

BRAIN BUILDER TIP Why not build on this by playing around with the idea behind this puzzle? Could you use it for a code, maybe? If you have problems remembering your credit card security number or your online banking access code, you could note it in this way. Say it is 4836: You could remember it as "square containing 1, square containing 2, triangle containing 1, and triangle containing 2." Or you could just have two symbols: a hexagon containing 8 (6 × 8 = 48) and a square containing 9 (4 × 9 = 36).

POINTS

PUZZLE 4 PILLOW SUMS

Since both of the long 7-digit numbers start with 5, the only number that can go in the first row across is 53378. Similarly, the only number ending in 7 is 38337, and it must go in the fifth row no matter in which order the 7-digit numbers are placed. The complete grid is below.

BRAIN BUILDER TIP Try fitting numbers together. Take a number sequence—say, the first forty prime numbers (2, 3, 5, 7, 11, 13, 17, 19, 23, 29, 31, 37, 41, 43, 47, 53, 59, 61, 67, 71, 73, 79, 83, 89, 97, 101, 103, 107, 109, 113, 127, 131, 137, 139, 149, 151, 157, 163, 167, 173)—and write them out with as many intersections as possible. Or note the birthdays of your family members or coworkers as a series of eight-digit numbers (month/day/year) and try to intersect these as many times as you can in a layout of your choice. Later try the second version of this puzzle (Puzzle 24, page 39) and see if you feel the benefit.

POINTS

• •

PUZZLE 5 ANTARCTIC NUMBERS

The answer is **343**. Here's the full sequence: $321 - 69 = 252$; $252 \div 3 = 84$; ¾ of $84 = 63$; $63 + 27 = 90$; ⅘ of $90 = 72$; $72 \times 5 = 360$; $360 - 17 = 343$.

BRAIN BUILDER TIP You can easily replicate this puzzle for practice. Say you take your current bank balance or your house/apartment/room number: Multiply by 4, add 256, divide by 2, take away 3, multiply by 2—what's the final answer? In my case, using my house number (124), the answer is 746. You may need to adopt the strategy of rounding up or down so that the answer is always a whole number—otherwise you may get lost in a world of fractions. Or you could try taking another angle on the problem: If the answer is 25 and the first number is 450, can you quickly devise five steps to get from one to the other? (For instance: subtract 150, divide by 3, multiply by 5, subtract 250, divide by 10.)

POINTS

PUZZLE 6 ARITHMARACE!

$$13 \times 5 = 65$$
$$\tfrac{4}{5} \text{ of } 85 = 68$$
$$98 - 54 \div 4 = 11$$
$$373 - 262 = 111$$
$$16 + 13 + 2 + 5 = 36$$
$$35 \times 3 = 105$$
$$140 - 74 = 66$$
$$23 + 59 = 82$$
$$15 \times 12 = 180$$
$$23 - 5 + 11 - 19 + 3 = 13$$
$$60 \div 5 = 12$$
$$23 + 55 = 78$$
$$23 + 23 + 23 + 23 = 92$$
$$876 - 765 = 111$$
$$12 \times 8 = 96$$

BRAIN BUILDER TIP How are your times tables? For some people it's worth spending 15 minutes or so to (re)familiarize yourself with them because they can speed up your mental arithmetic. Be on the lookout for addition strategies. It's often easy enough to add units, tens, and hundreds columns individually when the particular numbers are low—for instance, it's simple to add 1,321 to 2,433. You can get 3,754 by adding $(1 + 2)$, $(3 + 4)$, $(2 + 3)$, and $(1 + 3)$.

POINTS

NUMBERS **FIRST TEST ANSWERS**

PUZZLE 7 HOW MUCH ARE THEY WORTH?

A = 7, B = 4, C = 9, D = 16, E = 8, F = 2, G = 3, and H = 18, as shown below. You can see that F (2) is squared to make B (4), and B is squared to make D (16).

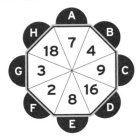

BRAIN BUILDER TIP Here's a game to build your familiarity with number relations. You might call it "number tennis." You play in pairs: Get together with a friend, your partner, a coworker, or one of your children. Let's say two friends, Arun and Joshua, are playing: Arun starts by giving a number (say, 23) then instructing "double it" or "times 2." Joshua gives the answer (46), then says, perhaps, "add 44"; Arun retorts with the answer, 90, and says "divide by 10." Joshua replies with 9 and says "add 101"—and so on. As in the Puzzle 5 tip, it makes sense to round to the nearest number to avoid getting lost among fractions with answers such as "17¾." (Or you could have a rule that giving an instruction resulting in a fraction earns a penalty.)

POINTS

PUZZLE 8 BID SERIES

Here's the completed grid. Only 5 can go directly above the 4 in the first column, and the 1 can't go in the second row (which has a 1 in it), so the 3 goes there with the 1 above it.

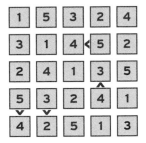

BRAIN BUILDER TIP Keep playing around with numbers and looking at the qualities and characteristics of different number sets. In some ancient cultures, perfect numbers (see the Brain Builder Tip for Puzzle 1) were believed to have magical or sacred powers. As we saw, a perfect number is one whose divisors (not counting itself), add up to the number itself. If the divisors add up to more than the number, it is called an abundant number. An example is 12: Its divisors are 1, 2, 3, 4, and 6—which add up to 16. Can you work out what the next two abundant numbers are after 12? *(Check the Brain Builder Tip for Puzzle 9 to see the answer.)*

POINTS

PUZZLE 9 GIVE US A SIGN

Here are the brothers' sums. Curiously, four of the five sums use the division function last.

4	×	8	−	5	÷	3	=	9
7	×	8	+	4	÷	6	=	10
15	÷	3	+	2	×	6	=	42
19	−	11	×	8	÷	4	=	16
6	×	7	+	12	÷	9	=	6

BRAIN BUILDER TIP Some people keep records of their everyday activities and consumption. They work out totals, averages, and ratios based on the figures. Whatever else you might say about this practice, it must be good for their mental mathematics. Do you drink coffee? How many cups a day? How many cups is that in a week? Do you ever miss a day—perhaps on the weekend? How much do you spend on coffee, say, in a week? What's that as a percentage of your weekly expenditure on snacks, lunch, and drinks? Or try this exercise with another daily expense—such as tea, or smoothies, or candy bars. *(Puzzle 8 answer: The next two abundant numbers after 12 are 18 and 20.)*

POINTS

PUZZLE 10 FARE'S FAIR IN NUMEROVILLE

The answers are shown below. In each case, the two italicized numbers, if added together, make the number shown in purple.

14 *24* 7 34 11 55 8 2 **97** *73*
($24 + 73 = 97$)
101 202 305 *69* 404 506 *32* 907 31 68
($69 + 32 = 101$)
39 41 53 63 82 93 124 118 *33* **72**
($39 + 33 = 72$)
3 2 *6* **30** 15 14 25 82 86 *24*
($6 + 24 = 30$)
791 917 717 919 *91* 19 999 99 **882** 1097
($791 + 91 = 882$)

BRAIN BUILDER TIP As with all the puzzles in this book, the best way to improve is to keep practicing and playing around with numbers—in particular, doing quick additions and subtractions. Here's a fun challenge: Draw a square and divide it into four segments; use any digit from 1 to 9 once only to create four numbers, two reading across and two down, so that all four numbers so created add up to exactly 100. For example, if you write 1 in the top left, 2 in the top right, 3 in the bottom left, and 4 in the bottom right, you will create these numbers: 12 and 34 across, and 13 and 24 down—making a total of $12 + 34 + 13 + 24 = 83$. Can you do it? *(See the Puzzle 15 Brain Builder Tip for the answer.)*

POINTS

PUZZLE 11 PUZZLING PEANUTS AT THE SHERLOCK HOLMES

Here is the completed grid. You'll see that the squares containing 1 and 2 must be in sequence because they're the only squares that can use the "one left, two down" step. From there, only a "one up" step is usable, landing on the 3, which reveals where you must be in the sequence.

	5		9
6	1	4	8
3		7	
2			

BRAIN BUILDER TIP To practice visualization, imagine a chessboard with one black piece and one white piece on it. The white piece makes these moves and the black piece does the opposite: 3 up, 2 right, 4 diagonally southeast, 3 down, 1 left, 2 diagonally northeast. Can you successfully visualize the squares where the pieces must start, and where they end up? You can check by getting hold of a real board and pieces and working through the specified moves.

POINTS

PUZZLE 12 AGENT 8

The answers are **4** (easy) and **12** (tough).

BRAIN BUILDER TIP Next time you have a few moments on your own, try playing this single-player version of the "number tennis" game I described in the Brain Builder Tip for Puzzle 7. This version is played with a single die. Start with the number 10. Throw the die. For each throw apply addition, multiplication, division, subtraction—in that order. Say the first throw of the die is 3, the second 4, the third 2, and the fourth 1: You would add 3 (10 + 3 = 13), then multiply by 4 (13 × 4 = 52), then divide by 2 (52 ÷ 2 = 26), then subtract 1 (26 − 1 = 25). And so on. As before, use a rule where you round answers to the nearest number to avoid getting lost among the fractions.

POINTS

PUZZLE 13 28 CAKES

Here's the completed Cake Mountain.

BRAIN BUILDER TIP Try playing darts. This is good for your mental arithmetic because you have to keep a running total of your score in your head (by deducting your total from the starting number—usually 501) and note possible double numbers that will let you finish. (As you may know, you have to end the game with a double or a "bull's-eye"—a dart in the center.) There are online versions of darts, but if you want to use the game as a way of improving your mental arithmetic, you may have to make an effort not to look at the onscreen score calculator. And of course the game's a good deal more fun when played with some friends.

POINTS

PUZZLE 14 IT'S ELEMENTARY

Each row and column in the grid should contain three purple squares and numbers that total 20. So space A should contain a purple square with a 5, B should be a purple square containing a 3, and C should be a gray square containing an 8.

BRAIN BUILDER TIP Here's another mental game for building confidence with number combinations and patterns: Imagine making your way across a regular black-and-white tile pattern like the one on a chessboard. Start with 2. For forward moves, double your total and for forward diagonal moves triple your total; for backward moves, quadruple your total, and for backward diagonals, multiply by 5. Then move in the sequence two forward, one backward, three forward diagonals, one backward diagonal. What do you get? (I get 4,320.) Now try it starting with 3.

POINTS

PUZZLE 15 TIME IN NUMBERS

Multiply the number of days in the week (7) by the number of hours in a day (24): $7 \times 24 = 168$. Add the number of weeks in a year (52): $168 + 52 = 220$. Multiply by the number of years in a century (100): $220 \times 100 = 22,000$. Subtract the number of minutes in a day $(60 \times 24 = 1,440)$: $22,000 - 1,440 = 20,560$. Add the number of months in a decade (120): $20,560 + 120 = 20,680$. Add the number of years between the present and the year 1000 (I'm doing the puzzle in 2013, so this number is 1,013): $20,680 + 1,013 = $ **21,693**. If you're doing the puzzle in 2014 then the answer will be **21,694**; in 2015 it will be **21,695**—and so on.

BRAIN BUILDER TIP How about these for a couple of brain-tickling number challenges: If Wednesdays were abolished and removed from the calendar, except every fourth one, which were turned into a Tuesday, how many Tuesdays would there be in a year? (Assume January 1 is a Tuesday.) If there are 380 calories in a strawberry donut and you eat three a day, how many calories do you get from strawberry donuts in a week? By my calculations, the answers are: 73 Tuesdays and 7,980 calories. *(Puzzle 10 answer: 1 in the top left, 2 in the top right, 4 in the bottom left, and 7 in the bottom right, creating 12 and 47 across and 14 and 27 down: 12 + 47 + 14 + 27 = 100.)*

POINTS

PUZZLE 16 NUMBER FITNESS

The finished puzzle is shown below. The first across entry must contain a 7 and 9; and the entry below it 6, 7, 8, and 9. The lowest sum you can make with those numbers without repeating is 13 (6 + 7), so that's what has to go in the first down entry.

BRAIN BUILDER TIP There are plenty of Kakuro books out there if you want more practice. Now try this: Give yourself a number—132, say—and work out what numbers divide exactly into it. Then consider how many combinations of those divisors can add up to that total. While we're thinking along these lines, note that there's a third category to add to perfect numbers and abundant numbers (see the Brain Builder Tips to Puzzles 1 and 8). When a number's divisors besides itself add up to less than the number itself, it is called a "deficient number." An example is 15: Its divisors are 1, 3, and 5, which add up to 9. The next two deficient numbers after 15 are 16 and 17. Can you work out the next two? *(See the Puzzle 17 Brain Builder Tip for the answer.)*

POINTS

PUZZLE 17 ODDS 'N' EVENS

NUMBER TIPTOE

The completed grid is shown below.

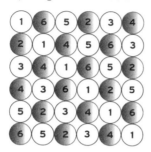

BRAIN BUILDER TIP Here's another interesting number thought: If you take a number that is evenly divisible by 9 and add its constituent digits together, the new number will also be divisible by 9. For example, take 99. If you add its digits up you get 9 + 9 = 18. 18 is also divisible by 9: 18 ÷ 2 = 9. This works with any number that can be divided by 9. The more you take an interest in number facts and connections, the more alert you'll be to numerical patterns and combinations in puzzles, and so the better your performance will be in the Second Test. *(Puzzle 16 answer: The next two deficient numbers after 17 are 19 and 21.)*

POINTS

PUZZLE 18 THREE-WAY FIT

The completed grid is below. In the bottom right chain, the 1 must be in the bottom row beside the 4 and the 6 because there's already a 1 in the row above, and the third and fifth columns contain 3's, so the 3 goes in the far right position. The 2 and 5 are in the other two places, but we won't know which order they're in until later.

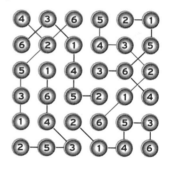

BRAIN BUILDER TIP Solving regular sudoku will help your performance with puzzles like this, though variants with irregular regions will help more. Our brain appears to be designed to develop and adapt to what is asked of it; this is why people can survive, and even thrive, in an urban, connected, and speeded-up world that's so different from the one in which we evolved many millennia ago.

POINTS

PUZZLE 19 NUMBER BY NUMBERS

The solution to our number Nonogram is revealed below. The encoded numbers are 569452.

BRAIN BUILDER TIP As I noted in *Brain Builder: Patterns*, the best way to improve at this type of puzzle is to try encoding some information in a grid yourself. Make a Nonogram of a simple image like a cross or a division symbol. More generally, boost your thinking by being on the lookout for new experiences and new tests of your visual intelligence and number skills. Try to maintain an inquiring mind. As you may know, the German-born physicist Albert Einstein, deviser of the special and general theories of relativity and a man widely hailed as a scientific genius, reputedly said "I have no particular talent. I am merely inquisitive."

POINTS

PUZZLE 20 WEIGH IT UP

The striped ball represents 1 pound, the white ball 2 pounds, the spotted ball 3 pounds, the pale solid ball 4 pounds, and the dark solid ball 5 pounds. Therefore, the left-hand side of the final scale totals 4 + 4 + 1 = 9, and three spotted balls (each representing 3) are needed to balance the scales.

BRAIN BUILDER TIP There's a good puzzle by the celebrated American puzzler Sam Loyd available called "Sam Loyd's Puzzling Scales," which can be easily found on the Internet. Loyd (1841–1911) was an American chess player, puzzle author, and recreational mathematician. Check out the book *The Mathematical Puzzles of Sam Loyd* by Sam Loyd and Martin Gardner (see Resources on page 92). Gardner (1914–2010), another great recreational math author who wrote the column "Mathematical Games" in *Scientific American* for more than 25 years, called Loyd "an authentic American genius." After trying the Sam Loyd puzzle, turn to Puzzle 27 (page 57) for a chance to see how you've improved.

POINTS

PUZZLE 21 SUM PEOPLE!

The faces represent 1, 4, 5, and 8, as shown, and the missing number replaced by the question mark is **18**.

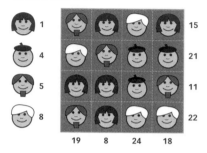

BRAIN BUILDER TIP This puzzle is a pictorial version of a concept in algebra called "simultaneous equations." If you're young enough that you haven't yet had an algebra class, puzzles like this will give you a leg up. Another way to play around with encoding and decoding is by taking a simple number/letter code—such as A = 26, B = 25, C = 24 … Z = 1—and writing your friends' names in numbers or your cellphone number in letters.

POINTS

PUZZLE 22 MAZE 4

The path through the grid is shown below.

36	22	78	70	30	40	12	13	52
40	94	96	80	16	54	30	77	72
42	74	48	54	76	64	44	68	92
60	56	28	22	98	86	18	22	36
80	69	12	30	40	36	32	62	52
84	78	20	88	24	46	72	50	64
92	38	22	90	66	34	96	34	70
16	24	32	28	50	38	76	16	56
22	46	14	82	94	82	62	26	88

BRAIN BUILDER TIP How familiar are you with multiples of 4? It may be useful to mentally run through the multiples of 4 up to 100, so as to have a few of the less familiar ones toward the top end of that range fresher in your mind. To help yourself more generally with puzzles like this, look at all your times tables or at lists of multiples for every number: Clearly, the more familiar you are with them, the more easily you will spot the numbers in puzzles like this. Another tip for numbers that you don't immediately recognize as being multiples of 4 or not is to subtract 40 or 80 from them; what's left should be familiar.

POINTS

PUZZLE 23 HAPPY 49TH AT THE NUMERO UNO

The finished grid looks like this. Note the 1-2-3-4 path discussed in the clue; if the 2 were one square lower, the path from 36 to 39 would be blocked after going from 34 to 36.

20	19	18	17	2	3	4
21	15	16	①	35	36	5
22	24	14	33	34	37	6
23	25	32	13	40	38	7
26	31	42	41	12	39	8
30	27	43	㊾	48	11	9
29	28	44	45	46	47	10

BRAIN BUILDER TIP Try creating your own Hidato puzzles. Every Hidato puzzle must have a unique solution, so learning how to avoid creating a puzzle with multiple solutions will teach you a great deal about how the paths work in puzzles like this, which will only help improve your solving skills.

POINTS

PUZZLE 24 MENU NUMBERS

The completed grid appears as shown below. Since both seven-digit numbers end with 743, the two across entries at the bottom must be the ones that end with 7 and 3.

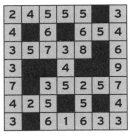

BRAIN BUILDER TIP A general tip for this type of puzzle is to start with the numbers that occur least frequently; in this case, that's the two seven-digit numbers. As with other puzzles, I'd also recommend creating your own version of a numerical crisscross, making sure that there's only one way of filling the grid correctly. Getting experience of the process from the other end will help you next time you're setting out to solve one.

POINTS

53

PUZZLE 25 IN THE ZONE

The diagonal clues really help you get started on this puzzle. The completed grid is below.

	17	19		17	11			
1	9	6	5	3	7	8	4	2
8	5	3	4	6	1	2	9	7
28 / 4	7	1	9	3	8	5	6	2 / 33
1	5	3	4	7	6	2	8	9
28 / 4	6	9	8	3	5	7	1	2 / 17
9	2	4	5	7	1	6	3	8
10 / 5	7	1	8	2	3	9	4	6 / 10
3	8	4	7	6	1	2	5	9
5	7	9	8	4	3	6	1	2

BRAIN BUILDER TIP Do you play checkers? If so, you're in good company! Checkers is the board game known in British English as "draughts." It will build your capacity for visual and sequential thinking and help you with puzzles like In the Zone. The game may date back as far as 6000 B.C.E. and was played in Ancient Egypt. It was first described in print in a book published in Spain in 1547. As we come to the end of the First Test, my principal suggestion is to repeat what I've written in several tips above—that if you want to get better at number puzzles, take an interest in numbers, number sets, combinations, and theories. There's an endless number of numbers just waiting to engage you.

POINTS

Remember the advice given earlier: Once you've completed the First Test, take a break and take stock—that way, you'll be ready to tackle the Second Test....

BRAIN BUILDER
NUMBERS

SECOND TEST

Are you ready for the Second Test? This section offers you a chance to try out what you've learned from the First Test and from working through the Brain Builder Tips and background information in the answers section to the First Test on pages 42–54. As before, there are twenty-five puzzles of varying degrees of difficulty—ten easy, ten medium, and five tricky. Good luck, and—once again—have fun!

PUZZLE 26 NOUGHTY CROSSES

This puzzle is part of a new TV quiz show, *Noughty Crosses*, which pits a team of teachers against a team of school pupils. It features an intriguing puzzle inspired by the game of tic-tac-toe (called noughts and crosses in the U.K.). The numbered squares around the edge of the grid tell you the number of Xs in all the boxes in line with the box that contains the number, horizontally, vertically, or diagonally (in either direction). Can you use these number clues to complete the grid so there is an X or O in every square?

3	4	3	3	3	7	4
5						4
3	O					2
3		X				6
4		X	O			4
6	X			X		4
4	4	3	4	4	6	3

Numbers down the sides have no vertical connections; numbers along the top and bottom have no horizontal connection; numbers in the corners have only a single diagonal connection. Some numbers along the edge have two connections and some have three; make sure not to forget any of the diagonals. This puzzle turns tic-tac-toe from a miniature strategy game to an examination of your numerical and visual sharpness.

BRAIN BUILDER CLUE The first 3 below the grid already has three X's in line with it.

PUZZLE 27 ON THE SCALES

Our butcher's assistant (Puzzle 20) creates a series of his coded brainticklers and publishes them in the butchers' trade magazine *Meaty Matters*. Can you solve this one? As before, each of the five different colored and patterned balls represents a different weight—1, 2, 3, 4, or 5 pounds—and your task is to work out which balls weigh what. This time you have to determine how many striped balls will balance the final scale.

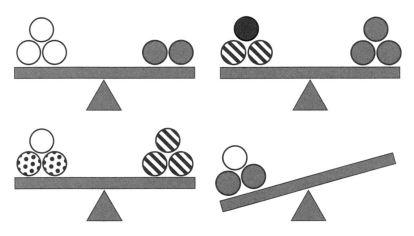

This number-code exercise will further develop your ability to think logically and to handle simple number combinations.

There's only one set of values that will work for the weights on the first scale.

PUZZLE 28 SILENT SUMS

Another day in the monastery, another puzzling sum for the monks to work out during their silent meal in the refectory (see Puzzle 9). Can you help them? You need to use the most common mathematical symbols ($+$, $-$, $\times$, $\div$) no more than once in each.

- Use three of the four symbols above in each problem.
- Don't create fractions or numbers less than zero at any step.
- Solve from left to right.

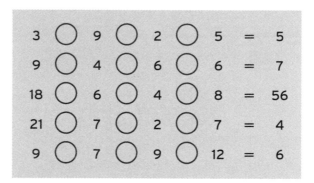

This is another lighthearted number puzzle—and one in which you'll benefit from familiarity with your times tables, and with common additions and subtractions, to speed up your calculations.

BRAIN BUILDER CLUE Over time the brothers have learned that the division function usually works near the start of the sum only if the first number is large.

PUZZLE 29 GARDEN GRID

A garden designer creates this tiled number challenge in the corner of a businessman's rooftop retreat. If you're a visitor, your task is to complete the grid so that the tiles bearing the numbers 1–49 connect in a consecutively numbered path through adjacent squares horizontally, vertically, or diagonally in any direction, starting and ending in the indicated squares. Some numbers in the path are already provided.

	42		44	4		
40		29				7
39	31		28	27		47
	①	32			㊾	
		25		21		19
	34		24	23	22	
35	12					17

Dr. Gyora Benedek's Hidato puzzles (see Puzzle 23) are an intriguing test of your visual and numerical thinking as you work out feasible positions for the available numbers. They are widely published in newspapers around the world.

BRAIN BUILDER CLUE There's only one way to get from 1 to 4, but then you must be careful with your choice of paths to 7. Remember to think ahead.

59

PUZZLE 30 BACK TO THE ANTARCTIC

Our mathematics and computing teacher's "Antarctic Numbers" game
(Puzzle 5) is designed so it's easy to enter new numbers and instructions for
her pupils to have another go. Here's a fresh challenge. As before, you take
the form of a penguin and start at the top left with the number provided: You
then work from one stepping stone to the next, applying the mathematical
instructions to the running total. What answer do you get?

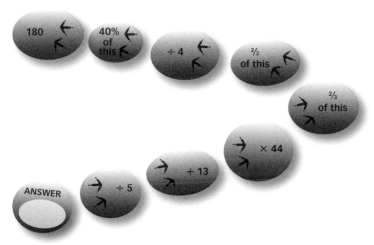

*Again, no calculators allowed! This will build your confidence with numbers and
simple arithmetic. Take whatever opportunities there are to do mental arithmetic
as you go about your day-to-day business.*

This puzzle adds percentages to the challenge. To quickly find 40% of a
number, try working out what 10% would be, then multiply by 4.

• •

PUZZLE 31 FINGERS ON BUZZERS …

You're quizmaster for your friends' general knowledge quiz. There are three teams of three players: Gold, Silver, and Bronze. Questions come in four categories—A, B, C, and D. Correct A answers are worth 4 points each; B answers are worth 3 points; C answers are 2 points; and D answers are 1 point. Wrong answers incur a one-point penalty, the total of which is indicated in parentheses.

Here's how to interpret the score sheets below. A score of 3A, 2B, 0C, 1D (–3) means that a player got three A questions right, two B questions right, no C questions right, and one D question right, but also got three questions wrong. Can you calculate the totals and work out which team won? Which teams came in second and third?

GOLD TEAM	
Player One	3A, 5B, 0C, 10D (–12)
Player Two	5A, 3B, 8C, 8D (–1)
Player Three	2A, 13B, 3C, 11D (–10)

SILVER TEAM	
Player One	3A, 3B, 3C, 20D (–12)
Player Two	4A, 12B, 5C, 1D (–17)
Player Three	5A, 4B, 4C, 12D (–0)

BRONZE TEAM	
Player One	1A, 6B, 11C, 11D (–3)
Player Two	5A, 5B, 3C, 10D (–2)
Player Three	1A, 3B, 4C, 13D (–0)

You may find this puzzle reminiscent of the fable of the tortoise and the hare … only simple arithmetic is needed, but don't rush. The most important thing is to avoid making mistakes. The total scores are quite close, so you could easily get the answer wrong with just a couple of small errors. This exercise tests and develops your mental agility and confidence with numbers.

 BRAIN BUILDER CLUE You may think the Silver Team is sure to win, since they have the highest total of 4-pointers and a good many 3-pointers … but will that be enough?

PUZZLE 32 A HEADY WAY WITH NUMBERS

Fresh out of art school, an intern at a fashionable milliner's comes up with the design for these funky numbered hats. To promote them she adds a number-puzzle element and her boss likes them so much that she keeps them in the final design for the display at the fashion fair. Can you work out the mathematical pattern the designer used? Your task is find the pattern behind the numbers on these pentagons and fill in the blank faces to complete the puzzle.

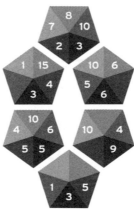

Confidence and facility with numbers are key elements of your everyday intelligence—your ability to seem smart and "switched on" at work and socially. Tests that require you to identify connections between numbers or among groups of numbers are often used in intelligence tests. Did you find this puzzle easier than the first time around (Puzzle 1)?

BRAIN BUILDER CLUE Start by investigating the relationship between the two places where faces touch at the top pentagon.

PUZZLE 33 SPACE SEQUENCE

On the space station, an astronaut takes a break from assessing numerical data to design a number-sequence puzzle for her coworkers. The arrows indicate whether a number in a box is greater or smaller than an adjacent number. Can you rise to this space-age challenge by completing the grid so that each row and column contains the numbers 1–5 exactly once?

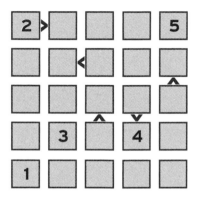

Compare this to Puzzle 8. Did you bring any new know-how from attempting that puzzle to this one? Using one of the simplest available sequences of numbers, this puzzle requires clear logic to assess possibilities.

You should be off to a flying start in the top row, because the arrows and given numbers provide all the information you need to fill all five boxes.

PUZZLE 34 AGENT 9

Here's a number-dexterity challenge from the video game "Agent 9," the sequel to the video game in Puzzle 12. As before, you start with the number given, then follow the sums from top to bottom to reach two answers.

Easy	Tough
4	**4**
Add 12	Multiply by 7
Divide by 4	Add 37
Add 23	Divide by 13
Divide by 3	Cube it
Minus 2	Plus 28
Multiply by 6	Divide by 9
Double it	Multiply by 7
Minus 3	Minus 23
Divide by 9	Divide by 12

Are you ready? Set? Then go! As I suggested at Puzzle 12, these exercises are more of a challenge when you're working against the clock. What about 1 minute for both columns? You're developing your speed of thought while building your mental arithmetic skills.

BRAIN BUILDER CLUE You may feel you're going around in a circle at the top of the Easy column.

PUZZLE 35 SPACEWALK SUMS

To keep alert on a space walk from the space station (Puzzle 33), an astronaut has to complete this sequence of simple sums, read to her over her headphones by a colleague. Can you help her?

$$98 - 27 \qquad 31 + ? = 65 \qquad 3 \times 16 \qquad 9 \times 8 \times 3$$

$$3 \times 9 \bullet 7 \times 18 \bullet 12 \times 5 \times 5 \bullet 13 \times 12 \div 6$$

$$9 \times 45 \bullet 15 \times 15 \bullet 67 - 34 + 89 - 101$$

$$43 + 54 - 85 \bullet 289 \div 17 \bullet 31 + 43 - 49 + 72$$

A little mental mathematics brings you focus and makes a good warmup before a more demanding task when you're at work or preparing to do some studying.

There are a couple of instances here where you can do a simpler calculation and double the answer. For example, you can work out 3×16 like this: $3 \times 8 \times 2$.

PUZZLE 36 THE LOGIC OF SUMMER LIGHTS

Stringing lights around his yard for a summer party, a philosophy professor has the idea for this number-logic puzzle. In the design he draws (below), some of the circles are shaded: Your task is to shade in more circles so that the number of shaded circles totals the number written inside the hexagon they surround. There's only one requirement: The shaded circles around any individual hexagon must all be connected to each other. (There may, however, be sections of circles separated from each other in the filled grid.)

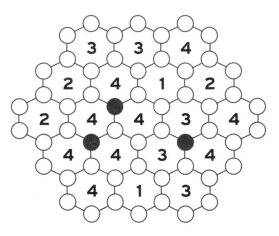

This provides a challenging test for your positional logic and clarity of thought. When solving, it may help to put a small dot into any circle you know should not be filled.

Note the 4 hexagon with two shaded circles around it in the middle row. Remembering that the circles around each hexagon must be connected, is it possible for the circle between those shaded circles to stay unshaded?

PUZZLE 37 FURTHER IN THE ZONE

Here's another of our tennis player's "In the Zone" challenges (see Puzzle 25). As before, your task is to place the numbers 1–9 once each in every row. Each arrow in the boxes outside of the grid tells you the total of the digits in the diagonal to which the arrow points.

- Numbers may appear multiple times in columns.
- Identical numbers may not appear in neighboring squares (even diagonally).

	12	27		22	11			
7	4		8			6		2
	2		9		5		1	6
3		7	5	1			4	2
4		3		6			8	
1	9		2		7	3		6
	8			5	4			1
2			8		5		9	
	4	7	5				6	
1	3		4	8	6			5

Clues outside grid: 30 (left, row 3), 28 (right, row 3), 16 (left, row 5), 20 (right, row 5), 11 (left, row 7), 8 (right, row 7).

This puzzle gains an extra level of difficulty from the fact that the vertical position of numbers in columns has no bearing. Like Puzzle 36 (opposite), this challenge primarily rests on logic, but it also requires basic arithmetic for the diagonal clues.

BRAIN BUILDER CLUE — Note what digits are missing in each row and see if they're present in the adjacent rows. For instance, the 9 in the second row eliminates two positions where the missing 9 in the top row could be.

67

● ●

PUZZLE 38 SUM MORE PEOPLE!

The workers in our health-food cooperative (Puzzle 21) took their colleague's puzzle and used it as inspiration for a set of posters displayed around town as advertisements. Here's one of them; can you solve the code? As before, each character represents a different number, and the number at the end of each row and column represents the sum of all the numbers in that row or column. Can you work out which number each character represents, and determine what number should replace the question mark?

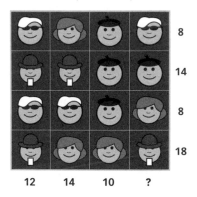

With puzzles like this it can help to note down solutions that are impossible and proceed by eliminating all except the possible answers. This approach has a fine pedigree: It was the one recommended by no less a figure than Sherlock Holmes. In his 1890 novel The Sign of the Four, *Sir Arthur Conan Doyle has his hero Holmes declare: "Eliminate all other factors, and the one which remains must be the truth."*

BRAIN BUILDER CLUE The top row suggests that the blond-haired worker with dark glasses must represent a fairly low number.

PUZZLE 39 NUMBER FITNESS 2

Here's another Kakuro (or "cross-addition") puzzle designed for our actress by her personal trainer (see Puzzle 16). Can you prove your number fitness by solving it? As before, the clues to this puzzle appear within the grid.

- Each blank square contains a single number from 1 to 9.
- Every set of numbers across or down has a total equal to that of its clue, shown either directly above or directly to the left (see the example grid on the left: 9 + 8 in the top line totals 17; 9 + 7 + 5 in the left-hand column totals 21—and so on).
- No digit may be duplicated within any set.

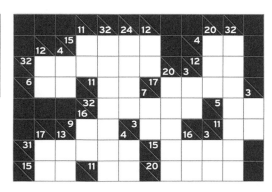

A Kakuro puzzle is just as satisfying as a crossword to solve, but because it uses no language it is a truly international logic puzzle.

Look for places where short combinations of squares intersect. One good place to start is the far-right 2×2 square where the vertical 3 clue crosses the horizontal 5 and 11 clues. Another promising area is in the upper left.

• •

PUZZLE 40 STAINED-GLASS ARITHMETIC

An up-and-coming student artist is having trouble with her design for a stained-glass window in the math faculty lounge. Taking a break, she devises this tricky 6×6 grid challenge. Each of the 36 squares in the 6×6 grid is filled with a single number from 1 to 9, with each of those numbers used exactly four times. Use the clues to complete the grid, bearing in mind that the same number must not appear in two horizontally or vertically adjacent squares. (Identical digits may be diagonally adjacent.) If the same number appears more than once in any row or column, this is stated in the relevant clue.

ACROSS
1 Two 1's; 8 is the only even number.
2 Two 8's; 5 is the only odd number.
3 Two 3's; no even numbers.
4 Two 2's; 1 is the only odd number.
5 Consecutive numbers placed in ascending order from left to right.
6 Two 9's.

DOWN
1 Two 2's; total of all six digits is 21.
2 Total of all six digits is 21.
3 Two 7's.
4 Consecutive numbers placed in descending order from top to bottom.
5 Two 6's; no 9.
6 Two 1's.

	1	2	3	4	5	6
1						
2						
3						
4						
5						
6						

BRAIN BUILDER
CLUE

The intersecting consecutive sequences in row 5 and column 4, combined with the limitations on odd and even numbers in the top two rows, give you a lot of information.

• •

PUZZLE 41 MATH MELTDOWN

Buoyed by the success of her bonbon number challenge, then the Cake Mountain for the math professor's party (Puzzles 2 and 13), our patisserie worker produces one more number pyramid, this time fashioned from scoops of ice cream, with the numbers added in chocolate sauce. Can you solve the challenge in 1 minute? The number on each scoop is the sum of the two numbers on the scoops underneath it. All you have to do is fill in the missing numbers and complete the three pyramids.

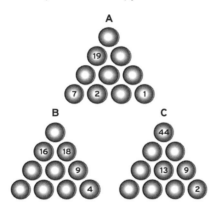

The position of several of the given numbers toward the top of the grids means that this time you definitely have to work down as well as up each pyramid to solve them. You'll be using and developing rapid-fire arithmetic. If this were a real-world puzzle, you'd have a different kind of time challenge ... namely, if you took too long to solve, the scoops would melt!

 Pyramid C looks well balanced.

. . . .

PUZZLE 42 FARE PLAY IN NUMEROVILLE

Here's another spot-the-totals number challenge that you have to solve
correctly if you want to keep your lucrative license as a taxi driver in the
video game "Numeroville" (see Puzzle 10). In each line of the number sheet
below, one number is the sum of two others. Can you spot each number and
its two constituents?

5	55	89	54	31	92	25	65	41	59
7	134	67	73	81	61	78	84	2	135
45	32	2	33	90	21	30	67	19	7
123	321	231	334	434	333	455	544	457	553
3	9	13	5	11	22	40	7	32	24

*This puzzle will help you read and combine numbers quickly. It's another
challenge for which you might want to set a time limit. In the video game there
is a 90-second time limit for all five lines: Do you think you can manage that?*

BRAIN BUILDER **CLUE**   For some combinations, it helps to scan the numbers and add the tens
and units independently.

PUZZLE 43 THREE-WAY FIT ON BROADWAY

Our playwright's work *Three* (Puzzle 18) transfers from London to Broadway and he writes a series of new three-way puzzles to circulate to the press for publicity. Here's one of them; can you solve it? There are three ways in which you must fit numbers into the puzzle: Each row, each column, and each set of linked circles should contain the numbers 1–6 exactly once each.

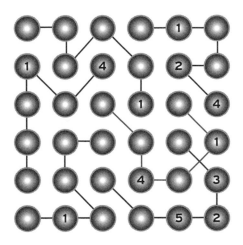

The more you practice sudoku-style puzzles, the better you'll become at doing them. Remember there are detailed tips on techniques and strategies for solving them available in books such as Puzzlewright Guide to Solving Sudoku.

You have enough information provided to complete the chain in the lower right corner.

PUZZLE 44 HOT-TUB NUMBERS

Back at the Puzzlers' Hotel (see Puzzles 4 and 24), the manager has now ordered laminated versions of his puzzles for guests to solve in the hot tub and steam room. Find the right homes for all of the numbers listed below the grid.

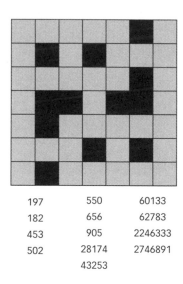

197	550	60133
182	656	62783
453	905	2246333
502	28174	2746891
	43253	

It shouldn't take much time to place the two long numbers and then—as before—apply numerical common sense to see how the other figures can be connected. How about setting yourself a 90-second time limit?

There are no five-digit numbers that can intersect with the end of the seven-digit number ending in 1.

PUZZLE 45 ONLY CONNECT

A scout leader devises this game to encourage the scouts to value their friends and relatives. The task is to draw lines connecting each pair of matching numbers, traveling horizontally or vertically (never diagonally) from square to square. The rules are:

- No lines may cross or otherwise pass through the same squares as another line.
- When completed correctly, every square in the grid will have been used as part of a connecting path.

9							4	12
					10			
					11			
	11	7		3			4	
					12			
2	8				5			5
					13			
		10				1	6	
		7		3	6	9	1	
2				8				13

This is a new type of challenge. The puzzle provides an engaging test for your visual intelligence and ability to plot simple connections.

There are some short and direct connections (between the 2's, for example) to get you started. Some connections are much more intricate and may contain more than one 90-degree turn. But remember—no diagonals.

PUZZLE 46 PAINTING WITH NUMBERS

An artist celebrated for her vast jigsaw canvases designs this jigsaw sudoku while waiting for a taxi to arrive. Can you solve it? Your task is to fit the numbers 1–7 into the grid in such a way that each row, column, and outlined section of seven squares contains the digits 1–7 exactly once each. She has included some numbers in the grid to give you a head start.

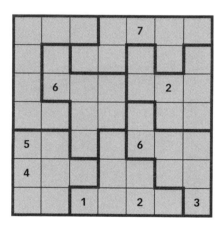

A number of the puzzles you've encountered in this book are intended to help develop the numerical and visual logic you'll need to solve this sudoku variant.

BRAIN BUILDER CLUE The fifth square in row 4 and the third square in row 6 must contain the same digit. Do you see why?

PUZZLE 47 POOL PILE-UP

An avid pool player comes up with this puzzle. The number in each circle is the sum of the two numbers in the circles underneath it. Can you fill in all the empty circles?

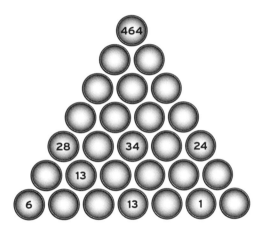

I like these simple number puzzles, which test your confidence with performing addition and subtraction quickly, so I've given you a good deal of practice in this book. Can you finish this one, which contains some quite tricky additions, in less than a minute?

 You'll want to start in the lower left and work your way across the bottom.

PUZZLE 48 NUMBER NUTS AT THE SHERLOCK HOLMES

Here's another tricky wrapper from the "Elementary" snacks at the Sherlock Holmes bar (see Puzzle 11), this time found on a pack of macadamia nuts. The task is to place the digits 1–9 in the white squares so it's possible to jump in sequence from one digit to the next, using only the steps indicated in the eight diamond shapes. The digits in each diamond indicate distance and direction traveled from one number to the next. For instance, the lower left diamond indicates a move one square up. One number is already placed.

- Each diamond step must be used exactly once.
- Both parts of a two-part step must be used, but may be taken in either order.
- No part of any step may pass over a shaded square.

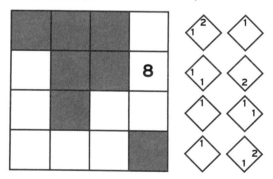

I find this a challenging test of logic and positional sense. All puzzlers have their own strengths and weaknesses, but practicing what we find hardest is always beneficial.

Both the upper left and lower right steps can only be used in one place in the grid.

PUZZLE 49 PUZZLES AT 30,000 FEET

This puzzle is given to all customers of Stay Bright Airlines as part of a package called "Stay Bright on Your Flight." The value of a shape is the number of sides the shape has multiplied by the number within it (so, a triangle containing a 4 would have a value of 12). Can you find a block of four squares—two squares wide by two squares high—with a total value of 50?

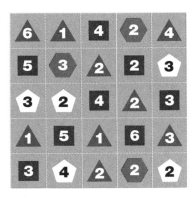

You may find you can solve this more quickly than the first time we tried this type of challenge in Puzzle 3. Did you try the follow-up tips (see page 43)? There's inevitably some trial and error involved. I find it speeds the process up if I pencil in the numbers represented by each shape.

Fifty's a high total, so you'll want to investigate shapes with more sides. Also note that you can disregard any 2×2 area containing an odd number of cells with odd products, since it can never have an even total.

PUZZLE 50 NUMBER SQUEEZE

After a rather cramped stay at a budget hotel, a traveler devises this Number Squeeze challenge while waiting for his train. How quickly can you fit the numbers in? The task is to fill the blank squares with whole numbers from 1 to 20, any of which may be used more than once. Some numbers may not be used at all. Multiple solutions are possible, so don't spend time trying to prove uniqueness; the goal is speed.

- The numbers in every row add up to the totals on the right.
- The numbers in the two long diagonal lines add up to the totals in the two black boxes.
- The numbers in every column add up to the totals along the bottom.

								93
13	7		14		9		1	**76**
12		2		1	3			**49**
	2		17			14		**84**
7	15		13	20	16	20		**111**
		16					3	**78**
16	5			9			2	**84**
		17			11		12	**87**
19		11		10			3	**100**
86	**47**	**101**	**115**	**82**	**79**	**110**	**49**	**96**

This requires meticulous cross-referencing. You'll need total concentration!

Start with the fourth row down, where only two numbers need to be found.

NUMBERS

SECOND TEST ANSWERS

As before, try not to turn to this section too hastily when you get stuck with a puzzle. Take a break, then attempt the puzzle again before looking up the answer. For clues, revisit similar puzzles in the First Test, along with the relevant Brain Builder Tips; then, by all means, consult the answers here. Don't forget to score yourself and compare your performance in the Second Test with how you did in the First Test. Then go to the other volumes in this series to test your thinking when it comes to puzzles involving sequences, patterns, and shapes.

Award yourself points as follows:
- Correct answer: **2 points** ● Wrong answer but on the right track: **1 point**
  ● Completely wrong answer or no answer at all: **0 points**

PUZZLE 26 NOUGHTY CROSSES

Since the 3 square pointed out in the clue already has three X's in line with it, every other square in line with that 3 can be filled with O's. Next, we can look at the 6 on the bottom. Two X's are in line with it diagonally, so four more must be in the column above it. Those four X's leave three X's unaccounted for by the 7 above the grid, which will be in the diagonal line shared by the 6 on the left side of the grid. Three X's on the 6's diagonal means there must be three X's on the bottom row, and we've filled two of its empty spaces with O's, so the remaining square is an X. Proceeding with logic like this will produce the full grid, shown below.

3	4	3	3	3	7	4
5	X	O	O	X	X	4
3	O	O	O	O	X	2
3	O	X	X	O	O	6
4	X	X	O	O	X	4
6	X	O	O	X	X	4
4	4	3	4	4	6	3

POINTS

PUZZLE 27 ON THE SCALES

This time the dark ball represents 1 pound, the white ball 2 pounds, the pale ball 3 pounds, the striped ball 4 pounds, and the spotted ball 5 pounds. Therefore, the left-hand side of the final scale totals 3 + 3 + 2 = 8, and two striped balls (each representing 4) are needed to balance the scales.

POINTS

PUZZLE 28 SILENT SUMS

The correct equations are as shown below.

3	×	9	−	2	÷	5	=	5
9	×	4	+	6	÷	6	=	7
18	÷	6	+	4	×	8	=	56
21	−	7	×	2	÷	7	=	4
9	×	7	+	9	÷	12	=	6

POINTS

PUZZLE 29 GARDEN GRID

The path from 1 to 7 must go along the top edge of the grid through the corner or you will eventually find yourself hitting a dead end when you return to that area.

41	42	43	44	4	5	6
40	30	29	3	45	46	7
39	31	2	28	27	8	47
38	(1)	32	26	9	(49)	48
37	33	25	10	21	20	19
36	34	11	24	23	22	18
35	12	13	14	15	16	17

POINTS

PUZZLE 30 BACK TO THE ANTARCTIC

The final answer is **73**. Here's how the sequence works: 40% of 180 = 72; 72 ÷ 4 = 18; ⅔ of 18 = 12; ⅔ of 12 = 8; 8 × 44 = 352; 352 + 13 = 365; 365 ÷ 5 = 73.

POINTS

PUZZLE 31 FINGERS ON BUZZERS …

The Bronze Team won with **135** points, the Silver Team was second with **133**, and the Gold team came in third with **131**. Here are the results in full:

GOLD TEAM		
Player One	3A, 5B, 0C, 10D (–12)	
	12 + 15 + 0 + 10 – 12 = 25	
Player Two	5A, 3B, 8C, 8D (–1)	
	20 + 9 + 16 + 8 – 1 = 52	
Player Three	2A, 13B, 3C, 11D (–10)	
	8 + 39 + 6 + 11 – 10 = 54	
Gold Team total: 25 + 52 + 54 = 131		

SILVER TEAM		
Player One	3A, 3B, 3C, 20D (–12)	
	12 + 9 + 6 + 20 – 12 = 35	
Player Two	4A, 12B, 5C, 1D (–17)	
	16 + 36 + 10 + 1 – 17 = 46	
Player Three	5A, 4B, 4C, 12D (–0)	
	20 + 12 + 8 + 12 – 0 = 52	
Silver Team total: 35 + 46 + 52 = 133		

BRONZE TEAM		
Player One	1A, 6B, 11C, 11D (–3)	
	4 + 18 + 22 + 11 – 3 = 52	
Player Two	5A, 5B, 3C, 10D (–2)	
	20 + 15 + 6 + 10 – 2 = 49	
Player Three	1A, 3B, 4C, 13D (–0)	
	4 + 9 + 8 + 13 – 0 = 34	
Bronze Team total: 52 + 49 + 34 = 135		

POINTS

83

- -

PUZZLE 32 A HEADY WAY WITH NUMBERS

The numbers on each pentagon add up to 30, and the numbers on facing sides of neighboring pentagons, when multiplied, also equal 30.

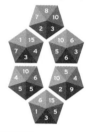

POINTS

PUZZLE 33 SPACE SEQUENCE

In the top row, only the 1 is lower than the 2, leaving only one space for a 4 (which is already present in the fourth column).

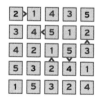

POINTS

PUZZLE 34 AGENT 9

The Easy column answer is **9**. The answer for the Tough column is **8**.

POINTS

84

PUZZLE 35 SPACEWALK SUMS

Here are the answers. (In case you're curious, the astronaut managed to stay alert and carry out a tricky repair job on an external camera.)

$98 - 27 = 71$ ● $31 + 34 = 65$ ●
$3 \times 16 = 48$ ● $9 \times 8 \times 3 = 216$ ●
$3 \times 9 = 27$ ● $7 \times 18 = 126$ ●
$12 \times 5 \times 5 = 300$ ● $13 \times 12 \div 6 = 26$ ●
$9 \times 45 = 405$ ● $15 \times 15 = 225$ ●
$67 - 34 + 89 - 101 = 21$ ●
$43 + 54 - 85 = 12$ ● $289 \div 17 = 17$ ●
$31 + 43 - 49 + 72 = 97$

POINTS

PUZZLE 36 THE LOGIC OF SUMMER LIGHTS

The circle noted in the clue cannot be blank; if it were, connecting the shaded circles would make a too-long chain of 5 circles. Shading that circle forces the opposite circle to be blank; the chain can no longer reach that far.

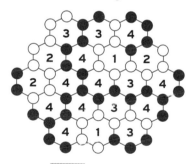

POINTS

PUZZLE 37 FURTHER IN THE ZONE
The completed grid is below.

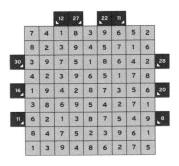

POINTS

PUZZLE 38 SUM MORE PEOPLE!
The faces represent 1, 2, 4, and 5, as shown, and the missing number replaced by the question mark is **12**.

POINTS

PUZZLE 39 NUMBER FITNESS 2
Note that if the values of the 3 clue on the far right were reversed, it would be impossible to complete the intersecting 11 clue.

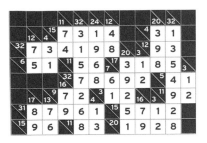

POINTS

PUZZLE 40 STAINED-GLASS ARITHMETIC
The top of column 4 can't be 5 (not enough digits to count backward to the bottom), 6 (only even number in the top row is 8), 7 (forces a 3 in row 5, which doesn't leave enough consecutive digits to the left), or 8 (a 7 can't go in row 2, where the only odd digit is 5), so it's a 9. That fills up column 4 and row 5—a good start!

	1	2	3	4	5	6
1	1	5	7	9	8	1
2	2	4	5	8	6	8
3	3	1	9	7	5	3
4	4	2	8	6	2	1
5	2	3	4	5	6	7
6	9	6	7	4	3	9

POINTS

85

PUZZLE 41 MATH MELTDOWN

By this stage of the book you're doubtless zooming through these simple arithmetic exercises quickly and easily. The completed pyramids are shown below.

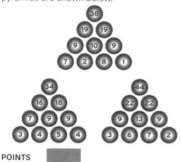

POINTS

PUZZLE 42 FARE PLAY IN NUMEROVILLE

The answers are shown below. The italicized numbers add up to the purple number.

5 55 89 *54* 31 92 25 65 41 **59**
  (5 + 54 = 59)

7 **134** 67 *73* 81 *61* 78 84 2 135
  (73 + 61 = 134)

45 **32** *2* 33 90 21 *30* 67 19 7
  (2 + 30 = 32)

123 321 231 *334* 434 333 455 544 **457** 553
  (123 + 334 = 457)

3 *9* *13* 5 11 **22** 40 7 32 24
  (9 + 13 = 22)

POINTS

PUZZLE 43 THREE-WAY FIT ON BROADWAY

The completed grid is below. In the group at the bottom right, the 1 must go in the leftmost circle because both of the other available positions already have a 1 in the same row or column. The 4 in that group can't go in the bottom row because that would place it in a column with a 4 already in place, which leaves the bottom row as the only place for the 6.

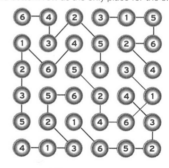

POINTS

• •

PUZZLE 44 HOT-TUB NUMBERS

Clearly, 2746891 must go down the left-hand edge because no other numbers end in 1. The completed grid is below.

POINTS

PUZZLE 45 ONLY CONNECT

The most convoluted connections are those between the two 9s and the two 10s. See the completed grid below.

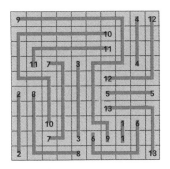

POINTS

PUZZLE 46 PAINTING WITH NUMBERS

The bottom three rows consist of three jigsaw areas, except for one odd-man-out square; correspondingly, one square from one of those areas protrudes into the row above. That protruding square's number must be the same number as the odd-man-out square. Neither square by itself has enough info to fill it in, but combined, we see they must contain 4's.

POINTS

PUZZLE 47 POOL PILE-UP

The completed number mountain is below.

POINTS

87

PUZZLE 48 NUMBER NUTS AT THE
SHERLOCK HOLMES

The steps indicated in the clue must refer
to the squares occupied by the 2-3 and 5-6
below (though we don't know those numbers
right away).

			9
3			8
5		1	7
4	2	6	

POINTS

PUZZLE 49 PUZZLES AT 30,000 FEET

Hexagon 3, triangle 2, pentagon 2, and square 4,
as shown: $(6 \times 3) + (3 \times 2) + (5 \times 2) + (4 \times 4) = 18 + 6 + 10 + 16 = 50$.

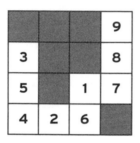

POINTS

PUZZLE 50 NUMBER SQUEEZE

As the clue suggests, the fourth row down is
a good place to start: You have to split 20 (111
minus the existing total of 91) between the
two empty squares. If you try putting 11 in the
farthest-right square, the other blank square
takes 9. This turns out to work well and helps
you complete the column on the far right, which
is now short by 17 and needs to fill two empty
squares. I continued by filling the grid as shown
below, but many other solutions are possible.
Before reading on, can you think of an easy
way to find more solutions? (I'll wait a moment
while you ponder.) Here's the answer: Find any
rectangle whose corners don't lie on either
long diagonal and don't contain any given numbers. You can then create another solution by
increasing one pair of diagonally opposite corners by whatever amount you like, and decreas-
ing the other pair of corners the same amount.
How many such rectangles can you find?

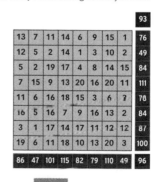

								93
13	7	11	14	6	9	15	1	76
12	5	2	14	1	3	10	2	49
5	2	19	17	4	8	14	15	84
7	15	9	13	20	16	20	11	111
11	6	16	18	15	3	6	7	78
16	5	16	7	9	16	13	2	84
3	1	17	14	17	11	12	12	87
19	6	11	18	10	13	20	3	100
86	47	101	115	82	79	110	49	96

POINTS

COVER PUZZLE SOLUTION

The numbers on each hexagon total 50, and the product of adjacent numbers is always 24.

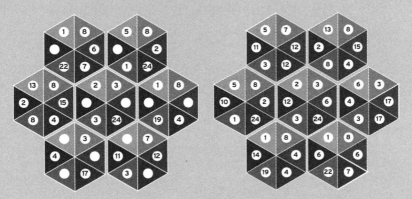

THE BRAIN BUILDER SCORING CHART

The *Brain Builder* series comprises four volumes. In addition to *Brain Builder: Numbers*, keep an eye out for *Brain Builder: Sequences*, *Brain Builder: Patterns*, and *Brain Builder: Shapes*.

Like *Numbers*, each of the other three books also contains two sets of 25 specially themed puzzles, the First Test and the Second Test. In the First Test, you measure your capacity for the particular type of thinking covered in that book, then set about improving your performance by taking advantage of the tips and guidance provided in the First Test answers before trying the Second Test.

You can use the chart below to record your scores in the First Test and the Second Test. I've included all four books in the chart so that, as you collect the titles, you can keep track of your scores and more easily compare your performances in different types of thinking.

Book	First Test Score	Second Test Score
Numbers	....	....
Sequences	....	....
Patterns	....	....
Shapes	....	....

What your score means

For each test:

- **40 or more**—an excellent achievement.
- **35–39**—you're doing well.
- **20–34**—you have a very good basis for improving.
- **Below 20**—don't be disheartened. We all have strengths and weaknesses in particular areas, but we all also have a remarkable capacity to learn.

Don't forget, these books are designed to help you improve! The other books in the series will help you test out and build on your thinking performance in different areas. Here's what it means if you show strength in …

- *Numbers* A strong performance in this book suggests you are clear-thinking, accurate, and confident in situations where you have to deal quickly with numbers.
- *Sequences* A good score in this book indicates that you have admirable visual intelligence and are strong in logical thinking.
- *Patterns* A high score here suggests that you do well looking for connections and are good at making sense of data.
- *Shapes* Doing well in this volume suggests you have excellent spatial intelligence and will perform effectively when you're required to present material visually.

Get your brain in gear

Do you know how powerful your brain is? You have 100 billion brain cells called neurons and each one can make connections with tens of thousands of others. And not only that—every single second your brain makes a million new connections among its neurons. So there's every reason to be positive and engage your brain. Keep up the good work!

RESOURCES

Books

How to Think: 50 Puzzles for Logical Thinking by Charles Phillips, Connections Books Publishing 2009

The Monster Book of Logic Puzzles & Sudoku, Nikoli, Puzzlewright Press 2010

Mathematical Puzzles of Sam Loyd by Sam Loyd and Martin Gardner, Dover Publications 2000

Maths Master: Making Maths Fun by Charles Phillips, Connections Book Publishing 2007 (published as *Logic Box*, Metro Books 2009, in the U.S.)

Proofiness: The Dark Arts of Mathematical Deception by Charles Seife, Viking Books 2010

Sam Loyd's Cyclopedia of 5000 Puzzles, Tricks, and Conundrums With Answers by Sam Loyd and Sam Sloan, Ishi Press 2007

The Moscow Puzzles: 359 Mathematical Recreations by Boris A. Kordemsky (translated by Albert Parry and edited by Martin Gardner), Dover 1992

The Number Mysteries: A Mathematical Odyssey Through Everyday Life by Marcus du Sautoy, Fourth Estate 2010

Websites

www.hidato.com
www.puzzlesociety.com
www.mathpuzzle.com
www.ageofpuzzles.com

DVD

The Oxford Murders, directed by Álex de la Iglesia 2008

π, directed by Darren Aronofsky 1998

NOTES AND SCRIBBLES

NOTES AND SCRIBBLES

NOTES AND SCRIBBLES

ABOUT THE AUTHOR

Charles Phillips is the author of 30 books, including the best-selling *How to Think* series, and a contributor to more than 25 others, including *The Reader's Digest Compendium of Puzzles & Brain Teasers* (2001). Charles has investigated Indian theories of intelligence and consciousness in *Ancient Civilizations* (2005), probed the brain's dreaming mechanism in *My Dream Journal* (2003), and examined how we perceive and respond to color in his *Color for Life* (2004). He is also an avid collector of games and puzzles.

PUZZLE PROVIDERS
Guy Campbell; Laurence May, Vexus Puzzle Design;
Charles Phillips; Puzzle Press